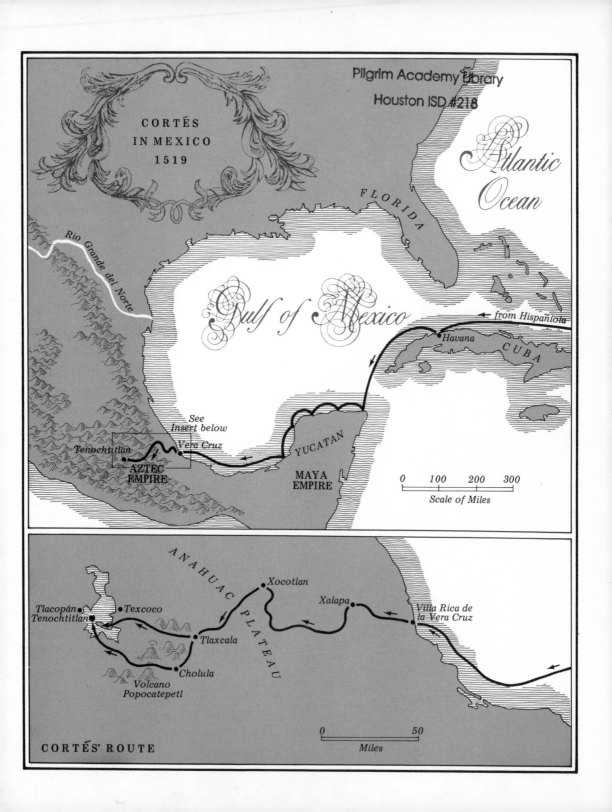

CORTÉS
IN MEXICO
1519

Pilgrim Academy Library
Houston ISD #218

Atlantic Ocean

Rio Grande del Norte

FLORIDA

Gulf of Mexico

from Hispañiola

Havana

CUBA

See Insert below

Vera Cruz

Tenochtitlan

AZTEC EMPIRE

YUCATAN

MAYA EMPIRE

| 0 | 100 | 200 | 300 |

Scale of Miles

ANAHUAC PLATEAU

Xocotlan

Xalapa

Tlacopán
Texcoco
Tenochtitlan

Tlaxcala

Villa Rica de la Vera Cruz

Cholula

Volcano Popocatepetl

| 0 | 50 |

Miles

CORTÉS' ROUTE

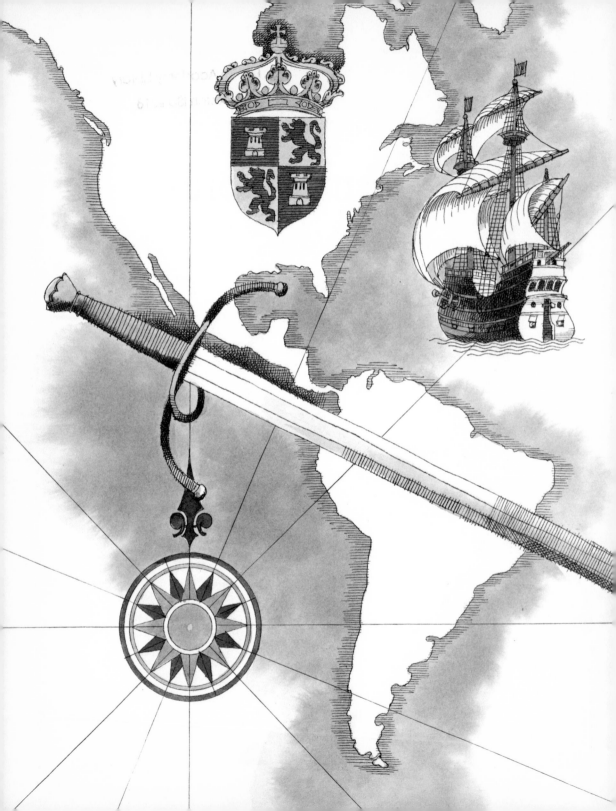

Conquistadores

By Meridel Le Sueur
Illustrated by Richard Cuffari

Franklin Watts, Inc., New York, 1973
A FIRST BOOK

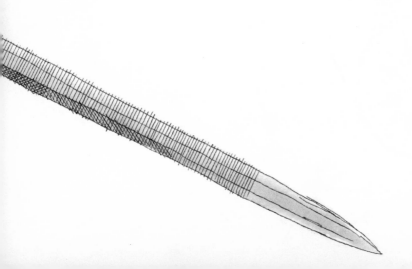

LIBRARY OF CONGRESS CATALOGING IN PUBLICATION DATA

Le Sueur, Meridel.
   Conquistadores.

   SUMMARY: Briefly traces the explorations of Columbus, Cortés, Pizarro, Cabeza de Vaca, and Coronado and
their effects on the civilizations of the New World.
   Bibliography: p.
   1. America–Discovery and exploration–Spanish–Juve-
nile literature. [1. America–Discovery and exploration–
Spanish] I. Title.
E123.L44   973.1'6   72-6051
ISBN 0-531-00744-8

Contents

1

The Earth
Becomes Global

In the fifty years following the landing of Columbus in the Caribbean, in what he thought was the Orient, an amazing and almost unbelievable adventure took place called the "Conquest." The handful of men who performed this amazing feat of opening the vast new continent to exploitation were called "Conquistadores."

It is almost unexplainable how they sailed in tiny ships, with few instruments of navigation over an unmarked and unknown ocean, to a forbidding and mysterious continent, and faced well-armed nations of millions. They "conquered" the vast empires of the Incas and the Aztecs, smelted down the wealth of gold they found there for their own sovereigns in Spain, and in a few years built their own cities.

They came from the Mediterranean world to an unknown land, ignorant of its vast size lying solid between two oceans and stretching from the Arctic Ocean to the tip of South America.

All the youth of that time had heard stories and rumors of mysterious lands, of the Fountain of Youth, of El Dorado full of gold, of the Seven Cities, and of seven bishops who had fled the Arabs to live in some far-off paradise. There were also terrible stories of islands peopled with pygmies and dragons, sirens, trumpet-blowing apes, islands with one-eyed men, men with pig snouts, monkeys that sang, people with double heads and blue skins.

It is hard to account for the amazing feat of the Conquistadores — a handful of men who marched into the unknown and changed the map of the world. Their exploits are surrounded by an air of improbability, if not unreality.

They destroyed two great empires, almost wiped out the people living there, burned their books, smelted down their jewelry and sculpture into gold bricks, and changed the history of the globe.

They sailed blindly into a world whose very existence was in question; they landed on the edge of an immense continent, seven thousand miles long, separating the oceans, and without a single water passage flowing east or west. They had to take their world with them — horses, guns, cannon, craftsmen, navigators, dogs. They loaded their tiny ships and set sail west.

They were swineherders, farmers, villagers, convicts, people who had never before set foot in a Spanish port. They were nobles, knights, and merchants, unaccustomed to any kind of physical hardship. The priests went to save souls from what they thought was barbarity and hell. All sought a utopia of gold and land and slave labor.

Eight hundred years of wars had impoverished their own land and had created the professional soldier and medieval knight. The crusaders now looked for new frontiers of wealth and adventure. All were filled with images of medieval chivalry, war, and power. Appearing in shining armor to the "dark continents," they saw themselves as half gods, bringing their message of salvation to savages.

Still it is hard to imagine them sailing in those little ships with their twelve cannon which they called the "twelve prophets," with their Toledo steel swords which could behead a man at one stroke, with horses and bloodhounds. It is hard to believe that they actually survived jungles, crossed high mountains, lived among animals and vermin and tropical heat. It is true many died. But some survived and explored this untouched wilderness carrying with them the standard of their sovereign and the cross of their Savior. They were required by their king and his investors to send back written histories of their adventures. It is hard to believe both their terror and cruelty and their indomitable courage.

These Conquistadores had no idea where they had landed, no idea of the extent of the land they had found or of its wealth, no conception of the intelligence, culture, and science of the people living there and of the vastness of their empires. The Conquistadores built their own cities over the ones that they had destroyed.

During Easter week of 1519 a young adventurer, Hernando Cortés, a lawyer-warrior-scholar, landed in the vicinity of what is now Vera Cruz, Mexico. He had an army of 508 soldiers, 32 crossbowmen who carried harquebuses, 16 horses, 14 pieces of artillery, and a navy of 14 ships and 100 sailors. In August he beached his ships on this unknown shore and went inland into the unknown country. Two years later the great city of the Aztec empire, Tenochtitlán, together with the empire itself, representing millions of people, was in his hands.

A few years later, Pizarro, a swineherder from the same village as Cortés, a man who could neither read nor write, arrived in Peru. With a handful of heavily armored men, he climbed the almost vertical mountains there and forced the emperor of the Inca empire to collect gold for him. He smelted down the gold and sent it to the Spanish queen. Pizarro then captured and cruelly killed the emperor, and began to build an empire of his own on the shambles of the one he had destroyed.

Cabeza de Vaca, a notary of Spain, had been shipwrecked and thrown up naked on the shores of the Gulf of Mexico. With two nobles and a black slave named Estaban, he walked across the lower part of what is now Texas and New Mexico. He ended at the farthest point of the Spanish empire, Culiacan, with a nation of dancing Indians following him into captivity. He is called the "gentle Conquistador" because there were no great cities on his route and therefore no wealth to be taken. He found something strange in the Americas — a wilderness of great beauty and a people with no sense of private property, who could not conceive that the earth could be owned, bought, and sold. He said he discovered something in them more enduring than gold. When they saw the misery of the stranded, naked, and shipwrecked white men, these Indians wept for them and, protecting them with their own bodies, carried them from fire to fire to their villages where they fed them and danced all night to cheer them.

Estaban became the guide for an expedition led by a monk to find the Seven Cities of Cibola. At the pueblo of the Zuñi he was mysteriously killed.

Coronado soon followed from Culiacan with masses of armored men to search for the fabled cities of gold. He went as far as what is now Kansas, found only the pueblos of the Tewa Indians and only the gold of corn. De Soto, who learned from Pizarro how to conquer, contracted a fever and died in the wilderness while looking for El Dorado.

Between the landing of Cortés and the end of the sixteenth century, some of the Conquistadores built fabulous kingdoms, killing off two-thirds of the populations. Their kingdoms lasted only a little while. Some of the Conquistadores were disgraced as Columbus was or denied the rewards of their strenuous lives. Some were killed as Pizarro was by rivals who coveted his empire as he had coveted the empire of the Incas.

But the Conquistadores changed the fate of the global earth. By their amazing exploits, greed, courage, and cruelty, they ended one cycle of the Mediterranean and African civilizations and started another on the other side of the globe. A new millennium began.

2

Columbus Reaches
the New World

In the fifteenth century there were maps available, but there were as many questions about these maps as there were empty spaces on them. The known world was very small. Some uneducated people still believed that the earth was flat and that one could fall off the edge. But the informed understood that it was round. The European nations were looking for new routes to the Indies and Africa. At great risk one inch would be added to the map as the Spanish or Portuguese sailed west searching for a short route to the east.

There was sharp rivalry between countries vying for the knowledge and conquest of this new space. Each nation tried to keep its navigational prowess secret. In Spain, death was the punishment for anyone who revealed any plan of the Spanish. Around the ports of the world there was much gossip and speculation.

One of the great men who developed navigation was Henry, prince of Portugal, called the "Navigator." He spent fifteen years sending ships down the African coast beyond the reefs of Bojador to get to Asia, but the northern trade winds

swept the square-riggers off course. Instead Henry's men colonized the Azores and reached the Cape Verde Islands.

Many considerations made Queen Isabella of Castile and the newly rich merchants willing to finance the expedition of Columbus to find a water route to the Indies. There was a general interest in establishing trade, heavy demand for spices, and a desire to conquer and Christianize foreign lands.

The young Columbus was seen in the towns, the countryside, at the court, and in the drawing rooms of the nobility discussing his ideas and raising moneys for the expedition. In the ports of Spain he talked to men, asking them to sail with him on this perilous journey. The terrors of the unknown seas were matched only by the terrors of the small, frail ships. Their bows, round and blunt, seemed to float upside down in the water, and buried themselves in every wave so the ships rocked like bowls. The heavy canvas sails pushed them down as well as forward, so that in a trough they were lost to sight.

The *Santa Maria* probably carried about a hundred tons and is believed to have been fifty feet long and eighteen feet wide. The *Pinta* was smaller and the *Nina* smaller still. Each ship had a pilot and a navigator. Many of the officers were sons of leading nobles. Crewmen were criminals let out of prisons, foreign tramps, cabin boys no older than ten, orphaned by the wars. They were to be paid seven dollars in gold a month. The nobles on board did not neglect the style of their dress, wearing their small sugar-loaf hats, slashed doublets of cloth, ballooning knee breeches, leather boots, swords, armor, and helmets. The crew wore simple leather jerkins. They were promised fabulous loot, trees hanging with gold and pearls, nutmegs bigger than grapes. Lured by riches they rarely got, they were eager to make this perilous journey. They made Spain the most powerful nation of that time, and most of them died poor and dishonored, in a world of fantasy.

From the harbor of Palos, Spain, Columbus set sail on August 3, 1492, amidst his cheering and weeping countrymen. The little wooden ships disappeared over the horizon, the crew fearful as they sailed into the unknown, into another world, another century.

The little horn lamp in Columbus' cabin swayed crazily as they waited for the sight of land or their own swift destruction. At last, October 12, came the cry of *"Tierra! Tierra!"* or "Land! Land!" as they saw at dawn the island of San Salvador. The fleet entered in a gap in the breakers and naked people appeared on the shore, astonished to see strangers arrogantly disembarking.

Lowering a boat, Columbus, with the captain from each of the other ships, the secretary, the king's accountant, and armed sailors, touched upon the new land, thinking it was the Indies. The royal standard-bearers planted the cross, the fleet's flag, bearing the crowned monograms of the king and queen. And the lord admiral took possession of the land saying the required prayers and pronouncements. Later he stated that the claim "should be for the increase and glory of the Christian religion and that no one should come to these parts who was not a good Christian."

The admiral thought the country was beautiful and the people "with very handsome bodies and very good faces." They bore no arms of any kind. He thought they would make excellent servants and ready Christians. He gave them little bells of

copper or brass, cones of metal, red cloth, and blue beads, and, in exchange, they gave him gifts, including some parrots.

The next day more Indians came out in their canoes and he noted their fine broad brows, their lovely eyes, straight legs, and that there were no fat ones among them. He looked closely for gold and still thought he had perhaps reached an island near Japan.

As they explored along the coastal waters every place looked lovelier than the last. He thought he would take back six Indians to show the queen. He went ashore to capture them and wrote that "the singing of little birds is such that it seems a man could never wish to leave this place . . . the flocks of parrots darken the sun. It is a marvel." He wrote to the queen that he believed, in all the world "there cannot be a people better or more gentle, full of love without greed, loving their neighbors as themselves, soft voices and they always smile." He told how they touched the Spaniards and kissed their hands and feet, and how generous they were, giving whatever they had for the poor things received.

Columbus had opened a new world to exploration, but he died believing he had reached a land with cities of spices and gold. He never knew the rivers of blood that would flow in the conquest of this land.

3

Cortés and
the Gold
of Mexico

It was February of the year 1519 when Cortés landed on the mainland of America. He had with him 508 men. They included 32 crossbowmen, 100 crewmen, and 20 chaplains. He also had horses, 20 greyhound dogs, a cannon, several brass guns, and enough powder and shot for all his men.

The governments set up by Columbus in the Caribbean had run into trouble. After his third voyage Columbus had been arrested and taken to Spain in irons. The government of the islands had failed. Chicanery, poor administrators, outright theft, had made a chaos of the colonization of the new land. Men looking for adventure made poor administrators. Many refused to work and looked for easy wealth. They had taken with them no surpluses and so were forced to live off the land. At first the Indians had welcomed and fed them but when their villages were plundered and they were hunted like animals, kidnapped to work in the mines, sickened with European dis-

eases, they literally disappeared into the hills. Slave-catching was a big business on the Caribbean coast.

The crown and the church still were interested in exploration but they also demanded gold, and the investors were withholding funds for future expeditions unless they got the promise of fabulous returns. One Spaniard who responded to this challenge was a genial, handsome fellow with a quick mind and a love of power, Hernando Cortés. He left Spain for the New World at the age of nineteen.

From Hispaniola he led an expedition to explore the mainland, landing on Yucatán, in February, 1519. Here he encountered his first Indians, the Tabascans. He fought them for two days, gaining the center of their town. A notary took advantage of a lull in the fighting to take possession of all lands within sight in the name of the king of Spain. Outnumbered hundreds to one, Cortés boldly declared his right to possess the lands, a right he would defend with sword and shield. When the native people ignored his claim and kept on fighting, he ordered his horses brought from the ships.

Riding at the head of his cavalry, bells ringing from the equipment of the horses, lances aimed at the naked bodies of the Indians, Cortés bore down on the frightened natives, who had never before seen a horse. They thought horse and rider were one, some kind of centaur, half man, half beast. The horses, combined with the fearful explosion of the guns, struck such terror into the Indians that they turned and ran. Now the Spanish held their town, having killed probably over one thousand Indians and having lost only two of their own number.

The army rested, and Cortés sent a message to the defeated chiefs demanding that they receive him. When they appeared before him, he gravely rebuked them for making war, telling them they deserved to be executed for resisting their kindly invaders. Render homage to his king, he demanded, and be of goodwill, and they would be received into his royal service. But his cannon was still angry, he warned them, and if they did not render their full submission, he feared it would leap forward and destroy them.

The next day the chieftains came again, bearing gifts: fowl, baked fish, flowers, and women for the conquerors. Among them was Marina who became famous as the concubine of Cortés and his invaluable go-between and translator. But above all, the people brought gold. For the first time, Cortés saw the fabulous gold that would lure the Conquistadores deeper and deeper into the new continent. Cortés accepted the gifts and the gold and made the Indians Christians, giving them a cross and an image of the Virgin.

When their wounds were healed, Cortés and his army set sail again, going along the coast in a great curve and dropping anchor on a reef in tropic waters. A bright sun shone on the mainland, and a fleet of canoes put out to greet them. Because it was Good Friday, April 21, 1519, Cortés named the city "Villa Rica de la Vera Cruz" (Rich Town of the True Cross). Here he was to hear for the first time of the Aztec capital, Tenochtitlán. In this distant capital, Montezuma, ruler of the empire, had already received a report from his spies of the flying ships that had landed on the coast. He sent five emissaries to invite the mysterious stranger, who he thought might be a god, to come to his city. They laid before Cortés gifts of gorgeous raiment which he was to wear, with a mask of turquoise, fans and rare embroideries of feathers enlaced with gold, and sandals of obsidian. The runners returned to their emperor and told him how they had been received.

They had been taken to the ships, they said, and had knelt before the captain. They had put on him the mask and robe and shield of shells and gold. They had laid at his feet the rare and beautiful gifts from their emperor and he had said, "Is this all you have to give? Are these your only greetings?" Then he had shot off a terrible cannon to frighten them and they had fallen into a faint. When they recovered he had fed them and told them to tell their emperor he wanted to come to his city to see how powerful he was. Then he had allowed them to leave.

They had drawings of the men in their bird boats, men with yellow beards and clothes of metal. They related how the men ate huge loaves of bread and had dogs with blazing eyes and panting tongues. How terrible was the smoke and noise and odor of their gun and how terrible when this gun shattered a large tree.

Then they handed to their emperor the glass beads and tawdry gifts they had been given, and told him that the captain had said his coming would be good fortune for them. Montezuma was filled with dread at this report and feared Cortés, believing him to be the Aztec god Quetzalcoatl, a deity with a fair complexion and a beard. Oracles had indicated that this god would return by way of the ocean. Montezuma steeled his heart for what was coming toward him.

A week passed and again ambassadors from Montezuma came to Cortés bringing more precious gifts. They spread the mats with objects of gold and jewels and were given in return three shirts, a glass cup, and "other things." They were also given long sermons by the chaplains demanding that they give up their idols and the practice of their own religion and accept the Christian religion.

By morning the ambassadors had fled back to their emperor, telling him their fears that these frightening strangers were planning to invade them. The Indians were bewildered by the lust of these men for gold. To them gold was important only to make beautiful things. They feared that their gifts of gold, far from satisfying Cortés, had only whetted his appetite for more. They were right. Cortés was determined to continue into the heart of Mexico. There he planned to capture the emperor and fill his boats with gold to carry back to Spain. Nothing would impede his search for wealth and glory.

Meanwhile, through emissaries from Cuba and Spain, Cortés heard of a plot against him by his rivals. Diego Velasquez, the governor of Cuba, had even secured an order for his arrest signed at the Spanish court. Since some of his men were involved in the plot, Cortés resolved to burn all his ships so the men could not return. He assembled his men and delivered a rousing speech quoting Caesar on crossing the Rubicon. He warned them of all the hardships ahead and then excited them with the promise of untold wealth and glory. And cunningly he got the men themselves to vote on beaching, stripping, and burning the ships they had come in, so there would be no possibility of turning back. Thus he was freed from sole responsibility for this daring action.

On August 16, 1519, leaving the charred hulks of their ships behind them, Cortés and his men began their hard journey inland. Dragging their artillery and supply trains, the heavily armed men climbed the mountainous land from matted jungles into vast terraces, toward the central uplands. Hacking, hauling, they went over slopes, escarpments, and through Indian towns abloom with gardenias and oleanders. If the local people offered resistance, they were frightened away by the explosion of the Spanish guns.

Then came the first great victory for Cortés. He learned how to apply in this new world the age-old tactic of divide and conquer. He learned that another group of Indians, the Tlascalans, were bitter enemies of Montezuma and they became his willing allies and informers. They told him about the great capital of the emperor, built on lakes, and entered by three causeways. In the city of Cholula, Cortés found more enemies of Montezuma who joined with him and the Tlascalans and they all passed over the mountains together until they saw the volcanoes and the valley of Mexico.

None of the military successes of Cortés would have been possible without the cooperation of these allies. They furnished the bulk of his infantry and manned the canoes that covered the advance of the brigantines across the lagoon of Tenochtitlán. They provided, transported, and prepared the food supplies needed to sustain an army in the field. They maintained lines of communication between the coast and highland and policed the occupied and pacified areas. They also supplied the raw materials and manpower for the construction of ships.

As this army moved over the mountains into the valley, Montezuma sent out emissaries to meet them. He offered them great tribute if they would come no farther. Cortés refused this offer and went steadily forward. In the words of a chronicler who had been one of the party, "they thirsted mightily for gold . . . they would stuff themselves with it and starve for it and lusted for it like pigs."

The chronicler, Bernal Diaz, describes the city of Tenoch-titlán, the site of present-day Mexico City, as Cortés and his army crossed the first causeway:

It looked like those enchanted things of which they speak in the book of Amadi because of the great towers and pyramids and buildings in the water, all of masonry. Some of our soldiers said that surely what they saw was a dream. These soldiers that had been in many parts of the world, in Constantinople and in all Italy and Rome said that they had never seen a square so well proportioned, so orderly, of such size and so full of people . . . . the markets had seventy thousand people daily come to trade in gold, silver, jewels, feathers, and tropical fruit.

Cortés himself wrote his king:

No tongue can describe the size of that great mosque for it is so great that in its orbit enclosed by a high wall a town of five hundred inhabitants could well be built. It contains delightful apartments where the priests live. The greatest of the many towers is higher than the church of Seville. There are many fine houses and gardens. I do not wish to say any more than that in its amenities and the bearing of its people there is almost the same manner as the people living in Spain and with so much convenience and order considering this people to be barbaric, and so far from the knowledge of God. It would seem to me well nigh impossible to tell of their excellence and grandeur and so I shall say not a thing about them only that in Spain there is not their like.

The drawbridges were lowered and Cortés, his army, and

his Indian allies, entered the city. How did this invasion appear to the citizens of this unfortunate city? From a rare manuscript of that day we have a description:

Four mounted soldiers came first and an advance guard rode back and forth peering into everything and examining everything. With them were the greyhounds, running ahead, sniffing everywhere. The bearer of the Royal Standard came next, ceremonially waving the banner from side to side. Upon the banner was the Castle of Castile and a golden lion. Now came the swordsmen with long blades. Then the mounted cavalry in quilted cotton armor and the jingling and rattling of the armor on the horses under spur and rein, sweating and frothing. The crossbowmen came next with crossbows and plumed helmets. Then came the armored charger bearing the Captain, his staff and personal bearers and behind them came their Indian allies, in the thousands, dancing, shouting and beating their palms, armed with their own weapons.

Captain Cortés, on the other hand, saw a procession two miles long coming to meet him, dancing to a two-toned drum, the jingling of conch shells, and the blare of trumpets, advancing in a lane of flowers, magnolias and cocoa blossoms, and on each side the lords robed in court dress of heavy embroidery and precious metals. On a litter in the center rode the emperor, robed and wearing golden, jeweled sandals, sitting among flowers, feathers, and wreaths. The two processions met and stopped. Marina came forward to translate.

"Arrive now in the land and rest, Lord," Montezuma said.

And Cortés answered, "Quiet your heart and do not be

afraid. We love you greatly. Now our hearts are satisfied we know him and hear him. At leisure he may hear what we have to say. . . ."

A sumptuous feast was spread before the invaders and again gifts were exchanged. A priest prayed, "Thanks to our Lord Jesus Christ."

The emperor then provided them with corn and grinding stones and women to cook for them. They were given chickens and other fowl and grass for their horses.

"All I possess is yours," Montezuma said.

Here they were, inside the city. But were they surrounded by friends or enemies? By accident Cortés' men came upon a sealed door and opening it they found treasures of gold plate and spun-gold fabrics. They sealed it up again marking it for future looting.

But it was all too quiet. News came that the emperor had ordered an attack upon the forces waiting in Vera Cruz and the men knew that they were in much danger.

Not letting on that he knew anything about this order, Cortés invited Montezuma to dinner in his own quarters. Once Montezuma was securely within the walls, Cortés announced that the emperor was his prisoner. He told the emperor that messengers had informed him how many Spaniards had been murdered on the coast at the emperor's command and that he would hold the emperor prisoner until the full truth be known.

"If you cry out," he said, "we will kill you."

Montezuma was horrified. His litter bearers were in tears. Marina urged him to accept his captivity. The emperor was put in chains and his chief nobles abandoned him in desperation.

As the days wore on and the rigor of Montezuma's imprisonment was relaxed, some of his leaders were incensed to see their emperor accepting his captivity, hunting with Cortés, playing games with him with gold pellets. Revolts flared up under the leadership of Cuauhtémoc but they were put down and the leaders put in chains.

Then the royal notary appeared before Montezuma and demanded his complete abdication. Montezuma, amidst the tears of his lords, commanded them to acknowledge their submission to the king of Spain and yield up tribute. He ordered his secret rooms opened and everything in them handed to Cortés. Greedily the men began melting down the beautiful gold objects into bars of gold more than three fingers wide.

At last, thought the men, they were to have the gold they had been promised and that they had risked their lives for. Cortés demanded of Montezuma that three empty rooms be filled with gold. Thereupon, night and day people came from the provinces laden with gold to ransom their emperor. Greedily the men melted the gold to take back to Spain. But there was never enough. Then the soldiers went too far, overturning the statues of the sacred beings of the Aztecs and rolling them down the temple steps, setting up in their place statues of the Virgin and the saints. The people of the city were outraged and felt that their gods had ordered the destruction of the Spanish army.

Meanwhile Cortés and his men slept in their steel armor, their horses saddled, never laying down their arms. Waiting was harder than dying. Then a messenger came saying a large fleet had appeared in Vera Cruz, on April 20, 1520. The fleet had been sent from Cuba by Governor Velasquez to punish Cortés with death, and a gallows had been set up for him on a hill above the harbor. Cortés marched back to Vera Cruz to confront this new enemy. He had no trouble defeating the general, Panfilo de Narvaez, who had come to kill him. Cortés took over his army, and in his orange-colored mantle woven with gold, he marched his army back to the capital, richer by five hundred fresh infantrymen and seventy new horses.

But when he returned to the capital he found that a terrible massacre had taken place. His Captain Alvarado had with no warning attacked a peaceful assembly of unarmed people as they danced in their temple at a feast of their god. Spanish foot soldiers had sprung upon the throng of priests, warriors, and celebrants from three gates at once, surprising them. They cut off the hands of the ceremonial drummer. They ran in with their swords stabbing the dancers so hundreds were wounded as they tried to flee. There were so many dead boxed in the temple that it was impossible to stand up for the bodies nor walk for the blood.

Across the city rose the cry of the outraged people and they swarmed into the streets fighting the Spaniards from house to house. Montezuma from a rooftop commanded them to stop and they called him a fool. Armed people were moving swiftly along the roads, entering the city.

Meanwhile reinforcements marching from the coast fought through to the garrison, pillaging and burning. Soldiers fought up the holy pyramid to the top and, covered with blood and wounds, hurled Aztecs down the steps. They swore they would not be defeated if twenty-five thousand Indians died for every Spaniard. The battle raged day and night. The causeways were destroyed.

On the sixth day of this battle Montezuma died under

strange circumstances. A rock struck him that might have been hurled by one of his own people. Cortés ordered prisoners to bear the body along the streets and bring it back to his people. They burned it on a pyre where "flame rose like the tassels of fire." And Cortés said he wept for him "as if he had been our father."

Now Cortés' company feared they would starve to death or die of thirst. Or they feared they would be wiped out by the enraged people who kept coming endlessly, and endlessly fighting. Cortés decided to withdraw. In a running battle he and his forces left the city and fled west. Cortés, it is said, worn with fury, exhaustion, and grief, leaned against a cypress tree and wept. The soldiers were unwilling to leave without their treasure of gold and loaded themselves down with as much as they could carry. Many were so heavily loaded that they sank in the canals and drowned. A bridge gave way and Cortés fell and was taken captive but at the risk of their own lives his foot soldiers rescued him, mounted him on a horse, and got him to safety with only a leg wound. This terrible night of flight and battle, June 30, 1520, has gone down in history as "La noche triste" (the sorrowful night).

The Indians pursued Cortés and his army. They came in fearful numbers led by the young and angry new emperor, Cuauhtémoc, killing many Spaniards whose bodies they burned nightly on the great pyramid. The snake drums and conch shells and trumpets sounded as the invaders fearfully watched their comrades burn.

The Spaniards were alone among a maddened people. The new emperor would not surrender. But their guns as well as their horses still made them a superior fighting force. And the tide of battle changed in favor of Cortés. Triumphantly he and his forces drove onward with their guns and horses. Cuauhté-moc was taken prisoner and killed, and the Aztec army retreated in panic.

Cortés now rested in the capital city of his allies. He gathered a larger army of Indian allies and reinforcements from Spain and began to plan an invasion of Tenochtitlán. Since the city was built on lakes, Cortés had thirteen ships built to use in his attack. The city's water supply was cut, and the battle was begun. The city was completely surrounded and cut off so that the inhabitants began to starve. In a final attack the Spaniards took the city and burned it. The war was over.

The soldiers now went mad for gold, ripped off the clothes of the people, seeking hidden objects in skirt or breechcloth. Young boys and girls were branded and initialed for ownership as slaves.

On August 13, 1521, the blood fires were cold, the waters of the lake were clogged with dead, and moving through this sickening stench, the conquerors had to press white linen handkerchiefs to their noses.

And the rain fell all night.

4

The Swineherder
Pizarro

The documents of Cortés describing the conquest of the Aztecs were published in Spain and circulated in many languages. They infected the entire western world with new dreams of wealth, of lost continents, and cities of gold.

Francisco Pizarro, a Spaniard of great energy and ambition, was one of those set afire by the conquests of Cortés. Pizarro was not a young man. Nor was he a nobleman. In fact he was a peasant, of illegitimate birth. He was not trusted by the new merchant noblemen and he had no influence with the court.

Pizzaro had sailed with Balboa when the Pacific was discovered and was on several expeditions that explored along the coast. From captured slaves he had heard stories of a vast inland empire covering what is now Peru, Ecuador, Bolivia, and northern Chile, all held under one powerful ruler. He dreamed of conquering this great nation and covering himself with wealth and glory. But how was he to pursue this dream? It was hard for him to muster money and men since he lacked the finesse and silver tongue of Cortés. But this difficulty challenged and inflamed him even more. To surmount his lowly position he was driven by a sense of mission, pride, honor, and a crusading zeal for gold.

Pizarro formed a partnership with Diego de Almagro and made a voyage from Panama in 1524 that was cut short by bad weather and hostile natives. Two years later they set out again, this time reaching and exploring Ecuador, where they found evidence of a great civilization. Pizarro and his men waited on the island of Gallo, while Almagro returned to Panama for provisions. Almagro's return was delayed by political interference, and Pizarro's men became restless. Pizarro gathered them together, drew a line on the ground, and said those who wanted to stay with him should step over the line. Sixteen men crossed the line and stayed with Pizarro. After seven months of suffering, and being able to do only limited exploring with a raft, Almagro arrived to rescue the group.

Unable to interest the authorities in Panama in sponsoring him, Pizarro went to Spain. On his arrival in Seville he was thrown into jail because of an old debt, but was soon rescued by the Spanish king, Charles I, who sent for him to report about the wonders he had seen in the New World. Charles was impressed and granted Pizarro rights to conquer, settle, and govern territory there. In 1530 Pizarro sailed to Panama and the next year set sail from there for Peru.

He had one piece of sheer luck. He had enlisted one of the country's best navigators. This man was able to take him down the coast of South America through the Humboldt current which flows north most of the year, making the passage, bucking contrary winds, slow and difficult. Because of these currents it had been five years since anyone had attempted to sail south from Panama.

They lay off the coast, waiting for a change of weather, in the coastal swamp Pizarro called the "Port of Famine." There they heard again vague accounts from natives of a powerfully organized kingdom of great wealth. Sick and hungry, they were spurred to push their luck to the edge of disaster and sail south again. They put out to sea instead of following the coast and came upon another swamp and jungle. There they launched their first thrust inland and from one village alone obtained considerable gold. Here Pizarro learned from people who had contact with the interior that he was on the threshold of a find that might be even greater than that of Cortés'. But they were forced back by the forests and the impenetrable jungles.

They sailed southward once more, crossing the equator, and beheld the promised land standing toward the south, its mountains towering in the tropical sun. They entered the Bay of Tumbes and the native people came alongside in their balsas to see the strange ships and exchange gifts. An Inca chief came aboard and invited them to the City of the Sun. He took leave of them full of wine and with the gift of an ax.

Pizarro was doing some reckless things. He allowed a bloody massacre at one village. At the city of Tumbes of the Sun Virgins the men looted and raped. But here Pizarro found the key to conquest that would unlock a great empire for him as it had for Cortés. He found that the Inca empire was threatened and split by rivalry between the ruler, Atahualpa, and his brother Huascar. Excited by the possibility of taking advantage of this civil war and gaining allies just as Cortés had done,

Pizarro left part of his force in Tumbes and marched into the interior.

Learning that Atahualpa was at the Inca capital of Cajamarca, Pizarro set out to visit the ruler there. The march was not an easy one and Pizarro knew well that the emperor could destroy them all as they crossed the mountains. To make matters worse, his men suffered from the high altitudes and could have offered little resistance at any mountain pass. What held the emperor's hand? Was the life of the Inca empire already running out?

It was winter in the Andes. The cold was intense, snow was on the ground. The horses suffered from frostbite. But the messengers who accompanied them along the excellent roads led them to halfway houses stocked with food and drink, and at each stop they were greeted with gifts from Atahualpa. Hernando DeSoto, a member of the expedition, went back and forth with messages and reports. And so, slowly, they crossed the mountains, an army of a hundred and ten foot soldiers, twenty men with a cannon, and sixty-seven horses. To this small, cold, and pitiful army DeSoto reported that Atahualpa was surrounded by forty thousand warriors. Pizarro sent him a message: "I make war upon no one or molest no one unless war is made upon me."

A day's march from the valley, distance runners trotted toward Pizarro carrying gold goblets filled with chicha, the potent Indian corn liquor. There Pizarro decided to camp and in the morning he looked down on the city. He marched his men to the outskirts, massing them in a great courtyard. They found the city had piped water and systems of sewage and irrigation.

Pizarro looked out from his camp and was appalled by the number of Indian warriors he could see. He sent DeSoto and twenty horsemen to meet the emperor who was sitting in front of his quarters on a small stool.

Atahualpa, about thirty years old, good looking, with a fine face and fierce eyes, was dressed in crimson silk. He spoke with the dignity of a great lord and made a profound impression on the Spaniards. Atahualpa and his warriors had never seen a horse before and as DeSoto, dressed in gleaming armor, wheeled and pranced his animal so close to the chiefs that their robes stirred in the animal's breath, the men flinched. They too thought they were looking upon a mythical creature, half man, half beast. DeSoto announced that there were thirty thousand men in camp and ten thousand more surrounding Atahualpa armed with pikes and lances. Atahualpa sent Pizarro a message that the following day he would come as Pizarro had come, with all his men fully armed.

No one knows, for history does not tell us how Pizarro accomplished his great feat of persuasion, but in some way he succeeded in convincing Atahualpa that his purpose was peaceful and that the emperor should bring his men into camp completely unarmed, adorned in their beautiful feathers, and meet him with flowers and dancing. How he lured the Incas into his trap no one knows, but the last moment of Inca power ran that day like sand in an hourglass.

Pizarro and his men waited. The waiting that fateful Saturday was awful for them all. Nobody slept that night for they knew they were outnumbered two hundred to one. Having decided to imitate Cortés and take the emperor prisoner, Pizarro concealed his troops in public buildings along the route of the

day's procession. They celebrated Mass that morning, chanting, "Rise, O Lord, and judge thine own cause!" Then they took their posts and waited. They waited for hours until at last they saw a magnificent and colorful procession moving in from the village. It stopped and then it began to move again in the bright cold light of morning. Women moved ahead of the procession sweeping the road before the Inca chiefs. Behind them came a bright multitude, singing and dancing, their crowns of gold catching the light. Then followed eighty or so chiefs, devoted to Atahualpa, who represented to them a glorious future. The watching soldiers of Pizarro saw this great glitter of gold and the countless numbers on the hillside. They could not tell if they were armed. Then came the litter of Atahualpa carried slowly among the people. His short hair was covered with golden ornaments and a large green turquoise flashed from his hand.

As they approached, Pizarro did not come forward to greet them. The golden litter of Atahualpa was set down and his attendants parted. Then a priest came forward with a Bible and a crucifix and gave a long sermon on the Christian faith which was translated and to which everyone listened courteously. He told of a king and queen in a far country of which the people had never heard and demanded that they pledge their allegiance to these monarchs and give up their pagan gods.

The friar, Vincente Valverde, is the only source we have for what happened next. He reports that he handed Atahualpa the Bible and the Inca chief threw it on the ground. The priest held up the crucifix and Atahualpa took it in his hand. "See this miserable god," he sneered, "killed by his own people!" Contemptuously he looked at these strangers urging him to renounce his own divinity in favor of the dead man on the cross, and pointing to the sun he cried, "My god still lives!" The friar picked up the Bible and returned to Pizarro.

The Indians began to talk to each other in Quechua and in the tension that followed Pizarro waved a white scarf that was his signal for attack. The guns roared and cut a swath of dead in the bright crowd. The hidden men reared out of the smoke crying the battle cry of Santiago and through the fire of the cannon the cavalry all charged at once, their swords of Toledo steel thrusting into the unarmed bodies.

The Indians died fighting with their bare hands. The musicians and dancers pressed against the walls, which fell under their weight. Those who were trapped in the square were slaughtered. The litter of Atahualpa had crashed to the ground and Pizarro had saved his life in order to make him his captive. The butchery continued even when the sun went behind the hills and the darkness deepened. Between two thousand and ten thousand Indians were killed. With Atahualpa captured the great Inca empire was wide open. Not a single Spaniard had lost his life.

Then Pizarro's soldiers went wild. Free to loot, they stole everything they could lay hands on. They seized five thousand women they found in the city and branded them, as well as the young boys, making them their servants. Every soldier had his own slaves. And they staggered, drunken, loaded with great vases of silver and gold, one alone worth nine hundred thousand ducats. They set themselves up in the homes of the men they had murdered; they ate and gambled, danced and made carnival all through the rainy season.

The storehouses filled up with gold that they rendered into ingots to be carried back to Spain. Whole herds of llamas

38

were slaughtered for meat and the herds further decimated for sport. They killed as many as 1,500 animals a day. They plundered army supply depots and granaries of stored wheat and corn.

Although the men plotted ways to defraud Pizarro, as usual the generals and nobles got the booty and the wretched soldiers very little. Meanwhile the men had to maintain themselves. Soon boots were needed more than gold and while gold was plentiful, it was not worth as much as a good Toledo blade or a pair of boots.

Now that they had received a ransom of all the gold available in the kingdom, DeSoto said that Atahualpa should be released. But Pizarro continued to hold him captive. He had dreams of becoming the rich governor of this domain as Cortés was of Mexico. Pizarro sent DeSoto away and set up his own court with himself as judge and prosecutor. And he himself delivered the verdict finding Atahualpa guilty of incitement to insurrection, the murder of his own brother, stealing gold for his family, adultery, and the worshipping of idols. In a badly written document he sentenced the Inca emperor to death by burning. Carried by torchlight to the stake, Atahualpa, fearing the destruction of his body, agreed to become a Christian for the favor of being garrotted. He was christened "Juan de Atahualpa" and then strangled. Even his request that his body be taken to his home was denied and he was buried in the new Christian cemetery, his women excluded from the burial ceremony. Only Pizarro attended, together with his officers, all in deep mourning.

When DeSoto returned he was bitterly angry, declaring

that Atahualpa should have been sent to trial in Spain as befitted his rank.

But Atahualpa was dead.

The massacre of Cajamarca had disgraced the Spanish forces in the eyes of the world and the assessment of history has not vindicated them. Pizarro had done the impossible. He had destroyed with his small force a fruitful empire and had put nothing in its place.

The queen of Spain gave Pizarro the governorship of the defeated empire. It was made a Spanish settlement with two of Pizarro's brothers appointed as judges. Administrators came in droves, dividing and destroying the empire among them, wiping out the crops and the irrigation systems, carting off rich minerals, creating chaos and waste and poverty. Pizarro quarreled with his partner Almagro and had him imprisoned and then killed. Other conspiracies and rivalries developed, and after eight years of this kind of "pacification" of Peru, Pizarro's rule was finally ended.

On a Sunday in June, 1541, Pizarro was at dinner with his captains. Followers of Almagro, including his son, consumed with envy and hatred, burst in upon the diners and attacked Pizarro. He defended himself according to historians, "until with weariness his sword fell out of his hands, and then they slew him with the prick of the rapier through his throat. And when he had fallen on the ground, and his wind failing him he cried unto God for Mercy, and when he had done so, he made a cross on the ground and kissed it, and then . . . yielded up the ghost."

5

Cabeza de Vaca, the First White Brother

"We seek passage, not dominion," Cabeza de Vaca said of his long journey of eight years around the Gulf of Mexico, through Texas and Mexico to the Pacific Ocean. He was accompanied by three companions, Andres Dorantes, a nobleman; Castillo, a student with a lyre; and a black slave named Estaban. "We are naked and unarmed. We are but four. We are the humble instruments of providence."

De Vaca and the others were members of the six-hundred-man expedition headed by Panfilo de Narvaez, the same general who had been sent to restrain Cortés and had failed in the attempt. Narvaez had gone back to Spain and then returned to the New World with five ships. Two ships were lost in a hurricane off Cuba, and the remainder of the expedition landed on the west coast of Florida in 1528. Narvaez decided that there should be exploration by land and sea, and so three hundred men stayed on land while the ships put to sea again. The expedition was never to be reunited.

The land group — Narvaez and de Vaca among them — marched along the Gulf of Mexico. After wandering inland, being harassed by Indians, suffering from disease and hunger, they returned to the coast and at Apalachee Bay they assembled all their resources to make five boats. With the iron from stirrups and spurs they made saws and axes. In their desperation they used the leg bones of horses for supports, fashioned bellows of deer skin, and made caulking from the resin of pines. They plaited the hair of horses' tails into ropes and rigging, sewed their shirts into sails. For food they ate their horses and raided Indian villages.

With these five boats the three-hundred-man group set out on the Gulf of Mexico, thinking to come by this route to the Pacific Ocean. After forty-seven days with forty of their number dead of starvation, they came upon a mighty river that flowed into the gulf. Not knowing that this was the Mississippi falling down a vast continent, they fought the river and its powerful tide but were pushed back into the gulf. Narvaez and most of the expedition were lost at sea, in November, 1528. But de Vaca's boat was thrown up by the surf onto an island off the coast of what is now Texas, and he and some eighty men survived. They were attacked by a band of Indians who tried to kill them.

After a winter of disease and hardship, only fifteen men were left. This group sailed to the mainland coast and then divided up, de Vaca and his three companions setting out together. At sunset of their first day's travel a strange thing happened that changed their lives. A group of Indians found them, and seeing the misery of the white men, they sat down beside them and cried. They howled in long lament for the suffering of their unknown brothers. De Vaca, writing a record for his king describing this adventure, said, "How strange to see these wild untaught men howl over our misfortune. Hearing them, I felt our calamity more." He further said that in his whole life he could not remember anyone weeping for his suffering, or for the suffering of other men, especially those unknown to them.

The Indians took the shivering men and covered them with their own bodies. Half went ahead and built fires at intervals, then returned and rushed them from bonfire to bonfire. They took them to their huts called "bohios," where they were warmed and fed fish and roots, and all night long the Indians danced and sang to allay the fears of the lost men and restore their courage.

Estaban soon learned how to talk to the Indians. Andres Dorantes, the young son of a Conquistador who had made a fortune in Peru, was not suited to survive in any wilderness without servants. Castillo was a student who played the lute well and had debated at the University of Seville on whether or not Indians were human and could feel the sensations and emotions of other people.

Cabeza de Vaca, whose name means "head of a cow," was tall, alert, and had been treasurer to the high sheriff of Florida. He had written in his dairy: "Will I return rich and noble? Will I see home again?" The four were taken in by the Indians who had rescued them and learned to know them and their ways. De Vaca wrote in his record for the king:

They have deep human feelings. They love children more than I have ever seen any people and they wept for us. They weep for the dead, not only of their own families but for all. They feed all children. They have nothing of value

45

but they live and cherish each other, singing and dancing.
They saved our lives. They spend all time and strength
to keep alive yet they have deep human feelings. We must
foster no despair. We cannot conquer the wilderness. We
must learn to live in it.

So Estaban mastered the new language and de Vaca became a
kind of trader, going to the gulf and returning with shells and
bones which he traded for things to eat. They moved frequently,
living off the land, following the berry crop and the cactus
fruit, learning to live in the new land.

Weary of this life, the four managed to leave this tribe,
and walking west toward the sun they fell in with a wandering
group of Indians who were thieves, liars, and drunkards. They
were a merry people, though, and Estaban taught them to
chant "Happy! Happy!" They had to cope with loneliness,
cold, hunger, and the terrible condition of not knowing where
they were or whether they would ever again meet up with other
Spaniards. Whenever they were unobserved they managed
to sneak out and away in the night. During the winter months
the Indians hibernated, and de Vaca and his friends almost
died of hunger and cold. They ate bark and dug themselves
into the ground for shelter. Sometimes they got separated and
had to wait for each other so they could continue west. They
thought that continuing in this direction they would finally
enter the Indian Ocean, but after several years of wandering,
they managed to get no farther than what is now Texas.

One day, finding themselves surrounded by a tribe of Indians, Estaban turned to his friends and said, "They want us
to heal them." De Vaca said in alarm, "We have no credentials.
We have passed no tests for healing." Estaban replied, "It is

our salvation. They think we can heal them. They will bring us food if we heal them."

De Vaca said a prayer and made the sign of the cross over the sick man the Indians presented to him. To his astonishment the sick man rose and walked away, seemingly eased of pain. He returned with venison, and other Indians, also bringing gifts. It was at this time that de Vaca wrote, "We seek passage, not dominion. We are naked and unarmed." Estaban said, "Between gods and slaves there is no difference . . . neither are human."

So they continued to pray and make the sign of the cross and Indians came from long distances bringing food and gifts. One day they brought a very sick man and laid him down before them. Estaban listened to his heart and thought him dead. He was terrified to treat him fearing that if the man were truly dead, they would all be killed. Of this experience de Vaca later wrote: "We are the humble instruments of providence. A man was near death. We thought him dead. We put our hands on him and wonder and fear spread among us all. He arose from the dead!"

Now the news did spread. They had become healers. They saw themselves in the eyes of the Indians as worthy administers of God's will. They had in a way become supernatural. As hundreds came with their sick, de Vaca advised his friends: "We must act as they expect us to act. They have made us their guardian spirits. We will model ourselves after St. Francis of Assisi with nothing for ourselves, our hearts open. And we must keep moving towards where the sun sets. That is our home."

So the Indians called them "children of the sun" and

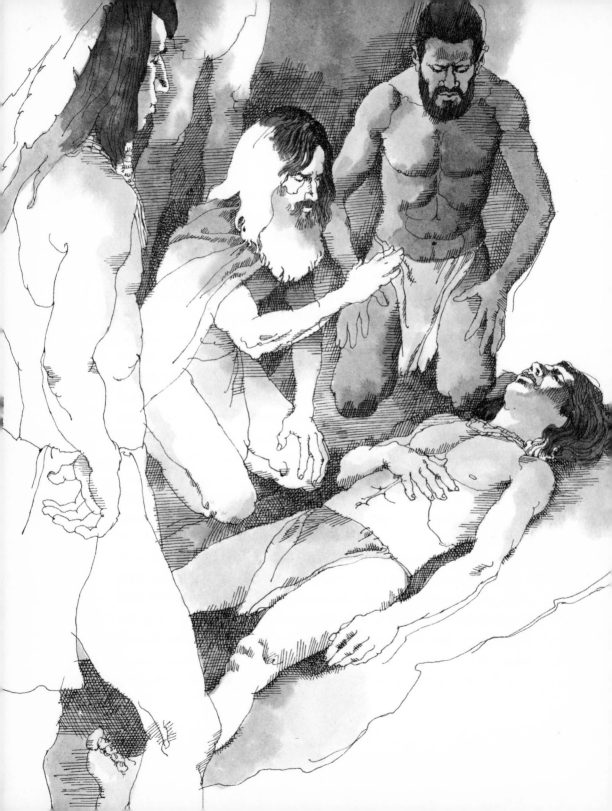

began moving west with them, even lifting and carrying them as they crossed the plains. A woman gave de Vaca a sacred gourd that had come down the river and they shook this gourd while holding the cross. And as this strange procession marched west, thousands more joined them in a wild, ecstatic throng, singing and dancing and striking their hands against their thighs, the air filled with piercing song and adulation.

Once the four Spaniards saw a sword buckle worn by one of their Indian hosts. He told them it had been left there by some people who had resembled them. But the Indian added, in body only, because these men had robbed them, taken their best men as slaves, and left their villages in ruins.

They then passed into the Pueblo country that is now New Mexico. It took them seventeen days to cross the desert into the valley of the Rio Grande, the people accompanying them all the way. In the Pueblos they found an agricultural people who did not wander, who had plenty of corn, and were potters and weavers as well. De Vaca saw they were people of good character and nature, capable of learning and changing.

As they turned southward, they found villages in terrible sorrow. Fathers had been taken captive. Children had been stolen as slaves, and the homeless were wandering and weeping for their beautiful ruined land. The marauders had been white men mounted on those terrible beasts of which they seemed a part, and they had pillaged and killed and left the land in ruins. The bereaved people begged the healers to stop the killing and the four men moved through the burning countryside with heavy hearts, touching and blessing the suffering people who followed them in hopes of getting their children back.

After this long trek of years, one day in 1536 they smelled

the ocean. They were approaching the coast near the further-most city of New Spain, Culiacan. The garrison there was amazed to see the four men, three of them white, one of them black, approaching, followed by an amazing throng of Indians — prospective slaves, walking into their trap. The soldiers were dumbfounded. They thought perhaps the three men were some kind of albinos.

But de Vaca stepped forward. "I am Cabeza de Vaca, treasurer of the high sheriff of Florida, under the grant given by Governor Panfilo de Narvaez." Solemnly he introduced his companions.

They had long been given up for dead. And here they appeared, followed by a wealth of prospective slaves, just as an expedition was being planned to find the Seven Cities of Cibola. The notaries came out to make certificates, record dates; administrators swarmed around the four men and their follow-ers. It did not take them long to appropriate the maize the Indians had been carrying for food. De Vaca and Estaban tried to get the Indians to leave before it was too late. Their Spanish countrymen suddenly looked evil to them. To Estaban it seemed that they had been in Eden and were now in peril. They were caught between Spanish rapacity and the devotion of the native people.

The governor tried to tell the Indians that de Vaca was a fake, that they were now helpless men in the power of the king of Spain, that now the power lay with the armed and the mounted. But the Indians gathered around their four friends and replied, "You do not speak the truth. They heal. You kill. They came to us naked and barefoot and without guns. You are clothed in metal and mounted on horses. They took nothing but gave all. You give nothing and rob us of our freedom."

De Vaca was seized and despite his blessing and bidding them farewell, the great procession dedicated to the Children of the Sun had been wantonly pressed into slavery.

The four men were taken to Mexico. They were not prisoners, but neither were they free. They had forgotten how to sleep in a bed, and clothes hurt their skin.

Castillo and Dorantes did not want any more exploring. De Vaca would not tell any mythical stories of the wealth they had seen, nor could he tell anything of the Seven Cities of Cibola rumored to be north in a new and strange country. He was harshly treated and finally in 1551 sent back to Spain in the hold of a ship. He died in 1557 forgotten by all except the Indians who had seen their first white brothers.

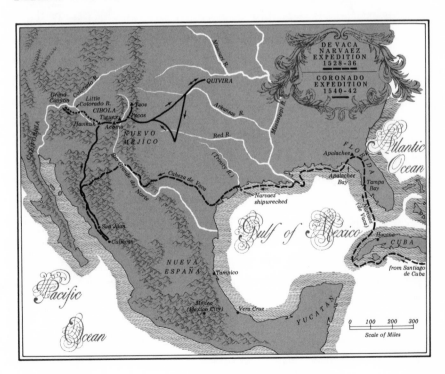

6

Coronado and the Seven Golden Cities

Spain needed another Mexico, another Peru.

Gold was needed to pay for the expansion of the Spanish empire in the New World. The future of thousands of ambitious men as well as of Spain itself depended upon finding new wealth to finance further expeditions.

People had long believed in stories about seven fabulous cities filled with gold and other riches. The Spanish had a legend of an eighth-century archbishop and six other bishops who had fled Spain when it was conquered by the Moors and had founded seven cities, called the Seven Cities of Antila. In the New World, Antonio de Mendoza, the viceroy of New Spain, heard rumors of gold in a region east and north of Culiacan. In 1539 he sent out a Friar Marcos and the former slave Estaban to search the area. Estaban was killed by Zuñi Indians, and Friar Marcos, afraid to approach their pueblo, viewed it from a distance and believed he saw a vast city. Indians had told him about Seven Cities of Cibola, supposedly

53

rich in gold, and Friar Marcos now concluded that the pueblo he saw must be one of these seven cities and that they were the same as the fabled Seven Cities of Antila.

Friar Marcos' report created great excitement in New Spain. Men poured into the capital from all over the province anxious for an expedition. As captain general, Mendoza chose Francisco de Coronado, a younger son of a well-to-do Spanish family. Coronado, born in 1510, had come to New Spain with Mendoza in 1535. He had married a beautiful and wealthy heiress and had carried out a number of projects for Mendoza. In 1538 Coronado had been appointed governor of New Galicia, in the north of Mexico.

More than 300 Spaniards and 800 natives were recruited within a few days for the expedition to find the seven cities. The recruits were mostly young men of good families, and there were three wives of Spaniards in the group. They took along their own livestock, in addition to 600 pack animals. With Friar Marcos as their guide, the expedition left Culiacan at the end of April, 1540.

Pedor Castanadas described the scene:

The young men curbed the picked horses from the large stock farms of the Viceroy. Each was resplendent in long blankets flowing to the ground. Each rider held his lance erect while swords and other weapons hung in proper place at his side. Some were arrayed in coats of mail, polished to shine like that of a general. Others wore helmets or vizored head pieces of tough bull hide. The footmen carried cross bows and harquebuses, while some were armed with sword and shield. When all of these started in duly ordered companies with flying banners, upwards of one thousand servants, and followers leading the spare horses, driving the pack animals bearing the extra luggage of their master, or herding the large droves of cattle. At the head of the glittering cavalcade rode General Coronado on his stallion of pure Arabian stock. The sun blazed against his gold plated armor, because of which he came to be known as "the gilded man." The white light flashed against his sword of finest Toledo steel unthrust like a challenge to the vaulting sky. He alone had a retinue of servants and twenty-two blooded horses for his own mounts. The cavalry followed and then the infantry. The air sparkled with festivity, sheep bleating, cattle bellowing, the little burros braying, herdsmen shouting and cursing, as they all passed before the royal Notary and put down the names, the number of men and animals, to report to the Crown.

Never did this glittering army suspect that many would die in the terrible desert trek that came to be known as the "Jornado del Muerto," the Journey of Death. Through five hundred miles of thirst, hunger, and death, many would die. They would suffer snake bites and the terrible heat of the day that would turn bitter cold at night. And all the while the Indians would be watching them and waiting for them.

As they passed away from civilization, they toiled for seventy-seven days across the desert. Many of them died and their bones became blanched in the heat. The animals died. The men trudged over vast flat plains and ate weeds in the wastelands. Mirages appeared before them of golden cities, and men died crying out for the gold they thought was beckoning them.

Everything Friar Marcos had told them turned out to be the opposite. Instead of cities of gold they found tiny mud huts.

They did find a city with Indians massed on its high walls. Weak and feeble, they attacked the city. Coronado was knocked off his horse during the battle but they managed to take the city which yielded what they needed more than gold — maize, beans, chicken, and salt.

But the Seven Cities of Cibola turned out to be seven little villages of mud. At this point Friar Marcos returned to New Spain. Coronado established headquarters, then he sent out scouting parties that discovered the Pueblo villages along the Rio Grande in the central part of New Mexico. The Tewa Indians received the scouts with flute music and ceremonials and gave them food and blankets.

These people were not warriors but farmers, who raised corn, beans, and melons. They dusted the soldiers with sacred meal and adorned them with feathers and flowers. In this village the Spaniards found an Indian prisoner whom they named "the Turk" and who might have been a decoy to lead them away. He told them fabulous tales about a river to the east, six miles wide, full of fish bigger than horses and boats holding forty oarsmen with golden eagles on the prow and great lords reclining under canopies of silk as they moved under trees whose branches dripped with gold bells.

Did he know what gold was, they asked the Indian. Of course he did, and silver as well — great vessels of silver were there in a city called Quivira. The listening soldiers wet their lips. One of them muttered he had seen the Turk talking to the devil.

But when winter had broken they headed east for Quivira, setting out across the buffalo plains of what is now Kansas, listening at night to the tales of the chained Turk. They

56

marched all summer and found nothing. Coronado left his force and went ahead with a small group. The men did not trust him, thinking he would horde the gold for himself.

But he returned with no news, having seen nothing but an endless plain under a hot sun, no river, no royal boats, no gold, only a naked king with a copper bangle around his neck. Coronado ordered the Turk killed, as they suspected he had plans to betray the whole army to enemy Indians. But the Turk to the end told wild tales of undiscovered gold, laughing at them all. Coronado thought the people he had seen, living off nuts, berries, cooking with cow dung, must not be the people of Quivira and that the city must be farther on. He thought that if they could keep alive another winter and go farther east in the spring they would surely find it.

Two days after Christmas, exercising his mount, Coronado fell from his horse and was struck in the head. He lay close to death. His confidence was now gone. Indians had attacked the garrison he had left on his route, so his return to Culiacan was threatened. He thought of home and wife. The search for the cities of gold had come to an end.

Coronado reached his home in New Spain again in June, 1542. Because of the failures of his expedition, he was removed from his office of governor. He died at the age of forty-four in Mexico City.

7

The New Race

Before the seventeenth century Spain governed most of the two
American continents. Three generations of Conquistadores had
discovered, subdued, and colonized the most extensive colonial
empire to that day. Nine years after Columbus had landed in
the New World, quick fortunes had been made, a vast empire
seeded. Gold and silver flooded Spain. Sugar, cotton, indigo
trade flourished. By 1540 thousands of slaves had been kidnapped, bought, and sold on the European and the New World
market.

The Atlantic Ocean became a road for a new mercantile
society. Europe that could not feed nor clothe itself now got
raw materials and slaves from the colonies, returned manu-
factured goods to new consumers, and a world commerce had
begun, competition in a world market. Immigrants also were
drawn from all parts of Spain to the New World. They became
farmers, merchants, producers. They brought women as part
of the colonization, but some Spanish men married Indian
women. Thus began a racial mixture of great strength. The
Indian women became the mothers of a new race. The African
slaves on the coast added another element to the mixture of

Spanish and Indian. Here in this vast valley of Mexico a common humanity encountered each other — the Indian, Mediterranean whites, Africans.

The Indians foretold a new race upon this continent. Despite the genocide practiced against them, many of them have survived, particularly in the mountains where they have preserved their culture and their language. In Mexico alone there are thirty-five different languages still spoken.

Here an America of the future has been planted despite the cruel fury, the ferocity of the Conquistadores' hunt for gold. There is a new race: some call it Indio-Hispana, and often simply *La Raza* or *Nueva Raza* — the new race.

Bibliography

Blacker, Irwin R. *The Golden Conquistadores*. New York: Bobbs-Merrill, 1960.

Crone, G. R. *The Discovery of America*. New York: Weybright and Talley, 1969.

Jameson, J. Franklin. *Spanish Explorers in the Southern United States*. New York: Barnes and Noble, Inc., 1959.

Merriman, Roger B. *The Rise of the Spanish Empire*. New York: The Macmillan Company, 1925.

Morison, Samuel Eliot. *Admiral of the Ocean Sea*. Boston: Little Brown and Company, 1942.

Prescott, William H. *History of the Conquest of Mexico*. Chicago: University of Chicago Press, 1966 (original edition 1847).

Stefansson, Wilhjahmus. *Great Adventures and Explorations*. New York: Dial Press, 1947.

About the Author

Meridel Le Sueur has taught at the University of Minnesota and done historical research on a grant from the Rockefeller Foundation. Born in Iowa, she now lives in Albuquerque and travels extensively in Mexico. Mrs. Le Sueur is the author of *North Star Country, Little Brother of the Wilderness,* and *Sparrow Hawk.*

Index

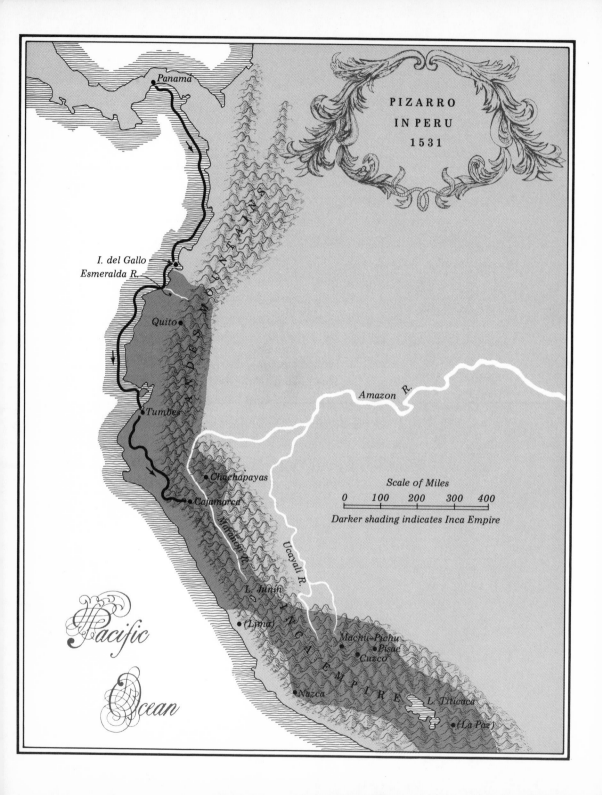

PIZARRO
IN PERU
1531

Panama

I. del Gallo
Esmeralda R.

Quito

Tumbes

Chachapayas

Cajamarca

Marañón R.

Amazon R.

Ucayali R.

Scale of Miles

0   100   200   300   400

Darker shading indicates Inca Empire

L. Junin

(Lima)

Machu-Pichu
Pisac
Cuzco

Nazca

L. Titicaca

(La Paz)

Pacific

Ocean

ANDES MOUNTAINS

INCA EMPIRE